DATELINE:
Jerusalem

Dramatic Dialogue Sermons
For Lent

Scott A. Bryte

CSS Publishing Company, Inc., Lima, Ohio

DATELINE: JERUSALEM

For more information about CSS Publishing Company resources, visit our website at www.csspub.com or e-mail us at custserv@csspub.com or call (800) 241-4056.

ISBN 0-7880-1936-8

PRINTED IN U.S.A.

To Kathleen, Xaq, and Meghan
and the People of God
at St. Mark Lutheran Church, Pittsburgh

Table Of Contents

Introduction

Dateline: Jerusalem is a series of six dialogues designed to present the familiar story of the death and resurrection of Jesus in a novel, engaging, and entirely modern way. Set up as a news interview program, *Dateline: Jerusalem* tells the story of the Passion from the points of view of six witnesses. Five of the six persons interviewed are familiar historical figures from the Gospels: Pontius Pilate, Caiaphas, Peter, Mary Magdalene, and John. The last character, the Centurion, is a composite of various guards and soldiers mentioned throughout the Passion narratives. As the premise of the series is that witnesses of the Passion are being interviewed on television, the two-millennia gap between their time and ours is largely ignored. Modern references are made throughout with an eye toward making their points of view more accessible to the contemporary mind. The persons interviewed tell the story from their own perspective, based on their participation in the events as described in the New Testament. The sequence of events in the interviews is generally the same as in the Gospel according to Saint John, although the Synoptic Gospels have been consulted as well.

How To Use This Program

Dateline: Jerusalem may be used during Lenten worship services, as part of a Christian Education curriculum for adults or confirmation students, as a youth program, and so on. Scripture lessons have been selected to accompany each. Each of the scripts is arranged so that the lines of the person being interviewed appear in **bold print**.

Ideally, the person being interviewed would appear on a television located near the interviewer. This can be done in either of two ways. First, the interviewee can be taped ahead of time, leaving gaps for the interviewer's lines. This is not recommended, however, as it is quite inflexible, and it may prove difficult to recover from even slight errors in timing. A more effective way, albeit one requiring a more elaborate set up, is to have the interviews done live via closed circuit television. This is not nearly as daunting as it may sound, and can be arranged rather simply using a home video camera and a VCR. If neither of these arrangements proves possible for your particular setting, the interviewee can simply appear seated at a table, or in a pulpit, and so forth.

Character Summary

The following are insights into the characters as written, and suggestions as to how they might be effectively portrayed. Please do not feel constrained by the suggested costuming and personality traits if they might be considered inappropriate for your particular setting, or if you have a better idea.

Pontius Pilate is depicted as a corrupt politician, and the only one of the interview subjects who says things that are intentionally misleading. Pilate can be clothed in a toga, or dressed in a modern business suit, with overcoat, sunglasses, and cigar. His name in Latin, Pontius Pilatus, is pronounced PON-tee-us Pee-LAH-tus (pronounce the "us" sounds as you would in the word "octopus").

Caiaphas the High Priest represents the largely disapproving point of view the religious authorities had regarding Jesus. More interested in power and maintaining the *status quo* than in the living word of God, Caiaphas has God firmly "in a box." Caiaphas has a smug, self-righteous piety, and peppers his speech with scripture quotations taken, for the most part, entirely out of context. Caiaphas can be dressed as a television evangelist, wearing a suit, gold watch, many rings, and slicked-back hair, with a large Bible open in front of him.

Peter, in keeping with his depiction in the Gospels, is portrayed as someone who does his thinking while he is talking. The dialogue rambles, with many asides. Peter's lines should be spoken rather rapidly. Peter can be dressed as a fisherman.

Mary Magdalene is bold and confident, and can be portrayed with an urban accent, or chewing gum. The pious legend of Mary's former life in prostitution is dealt with briefly in the dialogue and

9

dismissed as lacking any solid biblical evidence. It is therefore *not* recommended that she be depicted as a prostitute. She might best be presented wearing nondescript clothing or perhaps a veil.

John is very consciously depicted as the (future) writer of the fourth Gospel. Explicit mention is made throughout of John's concept of Jesus as the Word of God. This is the only one of the dialogues to contain scriptural quotations of any length. John might be portrayed as bookish in appearance, with glasses and a pencil behind his ear, perhaps seated at a typewriter or computer.

The Centurion dialogue makes very heavy use of the Gospel themes of Light and Dark, Hiddenness and Revelation. Since the Centurion is speaking on condition of anonymity, he should be shown in shadow or as a silhouette. This can be accomplished by placing him in front of a plain white background such as a bedsheet in a darkened room, with a small light source behind the Centurion, but in front of the background. The light sensitivity of the video camera will have to be adjusted so that only the outline of the Centurion and no details of his face are visible to the audience. If you are not using video equipment, the Centurion can be seated behind a sheet of light cloth or thin white paper, and a light placed behind him, so that his silhouette is cast on the sheet. The Centurion should be wearing a helmet.

Interview 1

Pontius Pilate

Romans 13:1-7; Luke 22:22-27; Luke 23:1-4

Good evening. As you have no doubt already heard, a routine exercise in criminal justice in the Roman province of Judea now has all the world talking. A self-taught rabbi and faith healer, a well-known public speaker in his early thirties who managed to amass no fortune and, in fact, had no permanent address, Jesus of Nazareth was executed by crucifixion, on a charge of attempting to overthrow the Roman Empire. We are privileged to have with us tonight, live via satellite hook-up, the man who brought those charges, Judea's Imperial Governor, Pontius Pilate.

Pilatus.

Yes, Mr. Pilate, "Pilatus" to you, too, and good evening.

Pontius Pilatus. My name is Pontius Pilatus, and it is early morning here.

Good morning, then, uh, Governor. Thank you for joining us.

I'm not the one who brought the charges.

Oh, I'm sorry, Governor, who did bring ...

(*Interrupting*) **Jesus was brought in to my office by the chief priest's personal security force.**

Is it normal for the chief priests to refer criminals to you?

11

If it's just a religious matter, a heretic they want to deal with, that's their business. If it's an imperial problem, they bring it to our attention. The mission of the Roman Empire has always been one of peace.

Excuse me, Governor, but the Roman Empire is well known for brutal treatment of its enemies, and for massacring or enslaving the people they conquer.

Yes, but peacefully.

What about the Jesus case made it an imperial concern?

Actually, nothing.

Nothing? I'm sorry, I'm not following you here, sir. Why was he brought to you then?

The chief priests initially sent word that Jesus was trying to overthrow the Empire, and that he was claiming to be a king himself, and that he was trying to organize a tax boycott.

On which of these charges did you have him executed?

None of them. I've seen revolutionaries before, terrorists, all those types. But this guy was no antigovernment wacko. I even asked him about the king thing, but I couldn't get a straight answer.

You mean about his being the king of the Jews?

I don't know what they were talking about anyway. Who cares what he said? The Jews already have a king.

A puppet ruler who answers directly to Caesar.

Herod Antipas was legitimately appointed by the Caesar to be the king of the Jews. This keeps them happy, and he doesn't give us any trouble. Besides that, he doesn't answer directly to Caesar. He answers directly to me.

If Jesus was not a real threat to the Empire, why did the chief priests send him to you?

Things get a little tense in Judea, especially around Passover time. You get people gathering in large numbers, they tend to get ideas. People who really are trying to start a war go to Jerusalem to stir up national sentiment. That's why I always make sure I'm there: to keep the festivities from getting too, uh, festive, if you know what I mean.

Terrorist groups plot the overthrow of the Roman occupation.

Exactly. And if the chief priests had gone after someone as popular as Jesus, people would have gotten all in an uproar, and that would have gotten my boys all excited, and it wouldn't have been pretty.

So that's why you decided to crucify Jesus.

This was never my decision. I had nothing to do with condemning Jesus. After the chief priests made their charges, which were ridiculous, they said that Jesus had been stirring things up in Galilee. I figured that made this Herod's jurisdiction. That's what we have him for; let him deal with it.

So you had Jesus sent to Herod Antipas. What did Herod think about Jesus?

Well, he was thrilled at first. He'd heard about him, and thought maybe he'd get to see Jesus do a trick — turn water into wine, or walk across his swimming pool — but he got nowhere. So when Herod couldn't get a show, or a straight

answer for that matter, he let his guards work Jesus over a bit, and then sent him back to me.

Yes, we've heard about that, and we heard that Jesus had been beaten by the high priest's guards before he was ever brought to you. Was he beaten by Roman soldiers as well?

No. We're the Roman Empire; we don't beat on people. That's uncivilized. He was flogged peacefully with a whip, but he wasn't beaten.

How do you flog someone peacefully?

The law prescribes forty lashes. We only did the tiniest fraction of that.

Oh, I see. How many lashes did he receive then?

From my men? A mere 39.

So, Governor, when Jesus was brought back to you, what did you do?

I dismissed the case. He wasn't really guilty of anything, except not knowing when to keep his mouth shut, and making the wrong enemies.

I understand that members of your family got involved in this case.

You leave my family out of this. They didn't have anything to do with it. My wife Claudia had a little dream, that's all.

What was the dream about?

It was about Jesus, not that my wife's dreams are matters for the public record. She said that I shouldn't have anything to do with him. She didn't offer any details and I didn't ask, just like you're not going to ask, understand?

Certainly, Governor. I apologize if I got into a sensitive area. If the charges were dropped, how is it that Jesus was executed?

Good. Now we're to the crux of the matter. This is why I agreed to come on your show in the first place, so that everybody could finally be completely clear on this. The decision to crucify Jesus was not mine, nor was it the decision of the Empire. I washed my hands of this once publicly already, but now I do so on TV. (*Dips hands in bowl of water, shakes them dry, then wipes them off with a towel*) **There, see? It's not my responsibility.**

But the order for crucifixion can only come from a Roman official, and the orders for Jesus' crucifixion, as reported in the *New York Post* this morning, do have your signature on them.

There is no way the *Post* or any of the media could get the real documents, but either way, it doesn't matter who signed the papers. It was the chief priests who pushed for it. They were actually threatening to report that I was not loyal to Caesar, which — Caesar, if you're watching — is certainly not true. My loyalties have always been in the right place. And then on top of that, they had the whole city standing in my courtyard, calling for Jesus' blood.

And I understand, the crowd was also calling for the release of another prisoner.

The mission of the Roman Empire has always been one of peace. I didn't want there to be a riot, for reasons I mentioned before.

There were too many groups in town looking to get the Empire out of Judea.

Exactly. Look for any excuse, especially around Passover. So I started this peaceful custom of releasing one convict, anybody they wanted, every year at Passover. Usually they pick somebody on death row. I was thinking I could use this to get around

the chief priests and get Jesus off the hook, but they thought ahead and had the crowd ready to call for the release of Barabbas.

You mean the rebel leader Barabbas?

No, I mean the terrorist Barabbas. George Washington was a rebel leader; this guy is a cold-blooded killer. He should be the dead one. I'd much rather have the king of the Jews running around free than this nut Barabbas.

Once again this issue comes up about Jesus being the king of the Jews. Didn't Jesus in fact claim to be more than a king?

Yes and no. When I pushed him on the king thing, he said his kingdom was not of this earth. Whether that means he claimed to be a king or not, I don't know. He kept talking about his Father, and though he never said it directly to me, the chief priests allege that he claimed to be the Son of God.

Do you think this could be true?

Now I'm quite the philosopher, but I'm not an especially religious man. I believe that the Emperor is god, of course — Tiberius, excellency, no doubt about it, you're a god in my book — but other than that, I stick to more ... practical matters. Still, I've heard all the stories about the gods coming to earth and having sons. I'm not ready to rule anything out as impossible. So I don't know where Jesus really came from. He wouldn't tell me when I asked. But I know he was not like any other person I had ever run into.

And that's why you made the sign.

Exactly. I had them put a sign on the cross that said *Iesvs Nazarenvs Rex Ivdeorvm*, "Jesus of Nazareth, King of the Jews." The chief priests had a fit, wanted me to tack *Clamat* at the

end of it, "Jesus of Nazareth, King of the Jews, or *so he says*." But, hey, I'm the Governor, I write what I want to write. Too bad for them.

We're almost out of time, Governor, but there's just one more thing we need to talk about. Jesus was buried under guard. What was that about?

This was the story that wouldn't end. Some guy asked me for the body so he could have a proper burial, so I gave him permission, after we made certain that Jesus was dead.

How was that determined?

Jesus quit moving long before the other prisoners being crucified that day, probably because of the beatings he got from the high priest's guards and from Herod's boys. One of my men poked him with a javelin, to make sure he was dead. When he poked so hard that the javelin went into Jesus' side a foot or two and he still didn't flinch ... well, I think that's evidence enough, don't you?

I should say so.

Then after he was buried, the chief priests asked for some troops to watch the tomb, so that Jesus' followers wouldn't come and steal the body and then claim afterward that he rose from the dead. I thought that was kind of far-fetched, but wouldn't you know, that's just what happened.

The body was stolen?

Exactly.

How could anyone steal the body with Roman guards outside of the tomb?

It was a long and boring assignment. The guards fell sleep. That's all I'm saying about it.

But if the guards fell asleep on duty, wouldn't they have been executed?

Well, ordinarily.

But they were not.

(*Getting more aggravated*) **I'm not at liberty to discuss imperial military policy with reporters.**

There are reports that you conspired with the chief priests to cover up the fact that there were no grave robbers, and that Jesus did, in fact, rise from the dead.

You know what, buddy? This interview is over. I'm not getting drug into this thing any more. I have nothing to do with this! Guards, arrest that cameraman! (*Image jumbles, then cuts out*)

Well, we seem to have lost the transmission. That's it for our interview with the Roman Governor of Judea, Pontius Pilate. Please be sure to join us next time as we continue to explore this fascinating story with an exclusive interview with the High Priest of Israel.

Interview 2

Caiaphas

Exodus 40:12-16; Hebrews 4:12—5:10; Matthew 26:57-68

Good evening. The execution of radical rabbi Jesus of Nazareth has made headlines far beyond the borders of Israel. What began as a power struggle among competing schools of Hebrew thought has now come to the attention of millions who are not at all familiar with the intricacies of Jewish theology. Here tonight to help clarify the matter for our viewers is the High Priest of Israel, joining us live via satellite from his office on the Temple Mount in Jerusalem.

Thank you for joining us, Annas.

How rightly the prophet Jeremiah spoke when he said, "His name will no longer be remembered." My name is not Annas. I am the High Priest Caiaphas. I am the one and true High Priest of Israel. Praise the Lord!

Oh, it appears our information is mistaken.

It's sadly out of date, friend. Annas, my father-in-law, used to be the high priest, and some people still call him by that title as a thing of honor, but the Lord called me to this office about fifteen years ago.

I would like to apologize for ...

Relax, friend. I wouldn't expect a godless pagan like you to know any better. As it says in the book of Proverbs: "The mind of a fool broadcasts folly."

Oh. So, how does one get to be the high priest?

Almighty God chooses the high priest each year.

Each year? Yet you said you have been the high priest for fifteen years now.

Yes. That is what I said, and I have truly spoken.

How can that be?

Well, clearly the Lord keeps choosing me. How truly wise is our God!

What exactly is the role of the high priest?

As high priest it is I alone who is the direct link between the Lord and his chosen people.

So you represent all the people of the world to God.

Not all the people, just God's chosen people, Israel.

I'm not sure I understand.

Well, of course you don't! But while you're sitting at home in your stocking feet drinking whiskey, watching Britney Spears videos, and playing on-line poker, we're over here living as the people of God — praying and reading the Holy Scriptures and following his commandments. Someone say, "Amen!"

Excuse me, Anna ... er, Caiaphas, but many of the world's people have laws very similar to the Ten Commandments.

Having heard of the Ten Commandments, or even trying to make poor imitations of them is not enough to bring you

along the paths of righteousness. And which ten commandments would you choose? The Lord has blessed his people with no less than 613 commandments, written in the law and the prophets.

Six hundred thirteen? How can people possibly remember that many laws?

They can't always. Satan, the Accuser, sometimes causes the people to sin and break the holy covenant of God.

What happens then?

Why, son, that's why the Lord has blessed them with me.

What do you do?

Why, I offer prayers and sacrifices to God on behalf of the people.

What kind of sacrifices?

The kind acceptable to God. The kind proscribed in the Holy Scriptures. Bulls, rams, doves.

To many of our audience, the practice of animal sacrifice quite frankly sounds repugnant. What does the slaughter of animals have to do with God?

Giving up something that you depend on for your livelihood, something dear and costly, is a way of giving a part of yourself. It is a way of apologizing for your sin. The blood of a perfect bull or a perfect lamb, the giving of its life, is how we obtain God's forgiveness for our sins.

So that is your job as high priest, to represent the people to God?

There's more to it than that. Once a year I enter into the Holy of Holies in the Temple, behind the temple curtain, into the direct presence of God.

What do you do back there?

We don't even tell the faithful all of it, only what is beneficial for them to hear. The temple curtain is very large and very heavy for a reason. It would be too much for anyone but the High Priest to be in the direct presence of God. For verily it says in Exodus that even "Moses hid his face, for he was afraid to look at God." So it is up to me not only to speak for the people to God, but I am also the voice of God for the people.

To say that you speak for God makes it sound like you have a rather high opinion of yourself.

I do have a high opinion of myself, and so do all the faithful. And so they should. Even God has a high opinion of me. I am the High Priest.

Are you saying that you are the one who really rules Israel?

No one as humble as I am would ever say anything like that. God is the one who rules Israel. I am nothing more than his spokesman, and the only one who can say what God wants for his chosen people.

What about King Herod?

Which one? There are two of them.

I'm sorry, I meant Herod Antipas, ruler of Galilee. And I thought Herod the Great had three sons.

Actually Herod had a bunch of sons; not sure how many myself. He had most of them killed to protect his own throne.

Killed one of them just a few days before he died himself. It says in the second book of Moses, "For I the Lord your God am a jealous God, punishing children for the iniquity of the parents." There were three sons left to divide up Judea. One of them, "Archie" - something, did a bad job of it even by Roman standards and they took him out and put their own man in — oh, it's got to be twenty years ago now. So there's only Antipas and Phillip left now of the Herod boys.

But then the two of them would be rulers of Israel.

The Lord rules Israel. The Herod boys are nothing more than Roman stooges, under the control of that wicked man Pilate.

But weren't you also appointed by Pontius Pilate?

Why, of course not! I'm a servant of the Lord, not the pawn of the Evil Empire!

But our investigative reporters have found that you were indeed appointed by the Imperial Governor.

Pilate had nothing to do with my elevation to the high priesthood.

Oh, wait. Fifteen years ago would be before Pilate was Governor. Then you would have been appointed by his predecessor, Valerius Gratus, correct?

(*Visibly shaken*) **I didn't come on your show to discuss politics.**

Then you are a Roman appointee?

If God wants to work through the Romans to appoint the right man to the job, that's God's business. I'm afraid I'm too busy to waste time talking about the Romans.

Yes, sir, we have gotten off the subject. Let's go right to the point you wished to make in so graciously granting us this interview.

I merely wish to point out, in all humility, that I single-handedly saved the world from God's terrible, swift sword.

Oh?

Yes. I (with God's help, of course) put an end to that rabble-rouser who was misleading God's chosen people.

You mean Jesus of Nazareth.

His name you know! You get my name confused with my father-in-law, but you rattle off the name of this heretic as easy as pie. These are evil times! It's a sure sign that the forces of Satan are running amuck in the world when this charlatan gets better press than I do!

What would Jesus do that you would call him a heretic?

What would Jesus do? What wouldn't he do? This man had no regard for the laws of God. He openly broke our commandments and spat on our traditions.

Caiaphas, if you could please give us an example.

(*Hesitating*) Yes. Although it goes against my better judgment, I will give you an example. I hope the good people of Israel will forgive me for some of the shocking and explicit things I am about to say. Most of what Jesus did shouldn't even be mentioned by God-fearing people. If there are any small children watching, please, in the name of all that's holy, I plead with you to leave the room.

What did he do that was that terrible?

He worked on the Sabbath.

The Sabbath? That's Friday night, right?

Over here we don't divide our days by random numbers on man-made clocks. When God causes the sun to set, the day ends and a new one begins. The Sabbath goes from sundown on what you call Friday, until the next sundown. "Remember the Sabbath Day and keep it Holy," says the Lord. It is a day of sacred rest. But Jesus treated it like any other work day.

You mean he didn't take time off from his carpentry business?

I don't know about that, but it wouldn't surprise me. What I'm talking about is he picked grain on the Sabbath and egged his friends on to do the same. But worse than that, he used synagogues, houses of worship, like they were his own personal doctor's office.

You mean he was healing people? We've heard some remarkable stories about what he could do. Wouldn't God want him to heal people?

Not on the Sabbath. Remember, I'm the expert here on what God wants. People were there in synagogue to be with God, not to be made well! They would have been just as sick the next day; he could have healed them then!

And so that's why you arranged to have him killed?

Doesn't anybody understand that it is better to have one man die for the people than to have the whole nation destroyed? No! His working on the Sabbath is not the whole reason. It's just the tip of the iceberg. He claimed to be the son of God. He claimed to be able to forgive sins. He passed himself off as the one person who could get you to God, and he's not. I am!

So, this is about jealousy?

It's about heresy. No one can forgive sins but God. It was like Jesus was saying he was God. That would give us more than one God. I know you pagans believe there are bunches and bunches of gods: Ba'al and Hathor and Elvis and the Teletubbies, but those are false gods. There is only one true God! It says in the sixth chapter of Deuteronomy, "Hear, O Israel: The Lord is our God, the Lord alone." Jesus didn't play by the rules; he didn't know his place. He had to go, and there's no two ways about it.

Then why was Jesus executed by the Romans and not by your guard?

It needed to be more public than we could make it. That, and since it was around the time of the holy day of Passover, we would have been forbidden from the work of the execution, and from handling the dead body. A corpse is an unholy thing.

When we spoke to Governor Pilate he said that he didn't find Jesus guilty of any capital offense.

Not to the mind of an ignorant Roman maybe, but we have a law, and according to that law, Jesus had to die. He committed blasphemy. If we had let him live, we would have been sinning. And the wrath of God would have come down on us all. God in his anger would have given us into the hands of the Romans. I had to act. I am the High Priest!

Governor Pilate tried to release Jesus.

Yes, and thanks be to God we were able to see that that Roman devil was going to try to undermine us. He asked the crowd what prisoner they wanted released, thinking they would ask for Jesus.

But they didn't.

No, before Pilate had a chance to come out and pervert their minds, we reminded the people that a good and pious warrior for the cause of Jewish liberty was rotting in Pilate's prison.

Barabbas.

Yes, Barabbas, now a free man, thanks be to God.

And Jesus?

Jesus is dead, as he should be. And now everything will go back to being the same as it always was.

You're sure that he's dead? We've heard stories that the tomb was empty.

Grave robbers. It's a sad and evil age when people can't even let heretics decompose in peace.

Grave robbers?

Probably the Romans did it, just trying to make life more difficult for us like they always do.

Thank you for speaking with us. But if I might mention just one more thing before we run out of time.

Certainly. I would be glad to enlighten you with God's holy truth.

Well, it's not that exactly. But we understand that there was an act of vandalism in the Temple on the day that Jesus died.

Yes, the temple curtain was torn in two, from top to bottom.

This is the curtain that only you are allowed to go behind?

The very one. But don't worry, we have turned it in to our insurance.

And they have agreed to replace it?

Not yet. We're having a little trouble with their investigators. They claim it wasn't vandalism.

What do they say it was?

They're calling it an act of God. What do they know? Why would God tear the temple curtain? Without that curtain, there is nothing separating God from the people. Act of God indeed!

Thank you, Caiaphas.

You're certainly welcome, my child.

Please join us next week as we continue our examination of the story of Jesus of Nazareth with an interview with the man Jesus called "Rocky": Simon, Son of Jonah. Thank you, and good night.

Interview 3

Peter

Habakkuk 1:14-15; 1 Peter 2:9-10; Luke 22:47-62

Good evening. We return tonight to the ongoing story of Jesus of Nazareth. What is it about this story that continues to fascinate and enthrall? Jesus, a former carpenter turned street preacher, was executed by crucifixion at the urging of a Jerusalem mob. Prior to that, Jesus had been a well-known and even well-loved figure in Jerusalem and all of northern and western Israel. He had, in fact, been welcomed into Jerusalem in an impromptu parade, the route lined with adoring fans, less than a week before his execution. Joining us tonight from an undisclosed location is one of Jesus' closest followers, a man who was with him right up until the very end, Simon, son of Jonah.

Hello, there.

Thank you, Simon, for being with us this evening.

Hi. Call me Peter. That's what most everybody else calls me.

Very well, then, Peter.

That's the Greek way of saying it, anyhow. Jesus and the other guys say Cephas. Means the same thing. Means "Rock." I'm not sure why they call me that. Kind of hardheaded at times, I guess.

Thank you. Peter, if we could talk for a few moments about Jesus of Nazareth.

Yeah, about that: it's not true, by the way. You know, not entirely, well, um, accurate if you know what I'm saying.

What's not true?

Well, I wish it were true, but it's not really, not technically, anyhow. I wasn't with Jesus all the way to the end. If by the end you mean his death, anyway, though it looks like that's not really the end of it, anyhow. I mean, you know, after his death, well, that's a different matter. But all the way up to his death — I was there most of the way. That little bit right before his death, and kinda during, I mean, no — I wasn't there for that, but a good 99.9 percent of the time, maybe 99.8, well, the rooster thing, may be 96.4 percent of the time ...

Why don't we back up a little bit? Could you tell us about your relationship with Jesus?

Oh, yeah. It all started a couple of years ago, maybe three years ago, maybe a little less, I'd have to see a calendar. Anyway, Andrew and I were fishing, that's my brother, I mean, Andrew. And Jesus called us to follow him. And what a time it's been since then, you'd never believe. The huge crowds and the wild things we saw. The miracles, people all messed up getting put back together right now while we're watching. And Jesus walking on water, and man, could he spot fish — just about ruined our nets. The stories I could tell you, I could talk your ear off.

I have no doubt. I understand that you were Jesus' closest friend.

Oh, sure, we're real tight. He even paid my temple tax for me one year. He said "Go down to the creek and pull out a fish and it'll have enough money in its belly to pay the tax for both of us." And I did, pulled out this nice big pike and slit it open; had two coins in it — weirdest thing. Jesus would come over to

the house, you know, help out, heal my mother-in-law or anything like that he could do. We got along real well. He called me "Satan" that one time, but that was my fault.

He called you "Satan"?

Well, not just like that. He could be real complimentary, too. He asked who we thought he was, and I said he was the Messiah, and he was real glad for me that I got it right, affirming and all that. "Right you are," he said. "And you are the Rock. And people saying that I'm the Messiah is the rock I'll build the church on." And I was all pleased with myself, but then he kept on talking. You know how some people do that? They just keep on talking? And he says he was going to be arrested and tortured and killed and that, and rise on the third day, and I didn't want to hear that kind of stuff, so I said, "God forbid," and that's when he called me "Satan."

I'm sorry, I don't see the connection. Why would he call you "Satan" for not wanting him to suffer?

"Get behind me, Satan," is what he said. "You're thinking like people think, not like God thinks." Turns out that he was right about that, just like he was right about everything else.

You mean about your being Satan?

No, no. Gee, I hope not. No, he was right about the suffering and dying part, and the rest of it, too. That's just what happened.

You said that you weren't with Jesus at the very end. What happened?

Well, we were sitting down to dinner together, leaning down to dinner really, you know how people do. It was Passover, the Seder. It's the last meal we had together (well, until recently)

31

and Jesus said that one of us was going to betray him. We all wanted Jesus to know it wasn't going to be us. I said, "Even if I have to die for you, I'm not going to betray you, ever." Everybody else said that, too. But Jesus told me that I would let him down three times, right then, before the next morning. Like stabbing me in the heart with a knife. That hurt worse than being called Satan. I couldn't believe he didn't trust me better than that, after all that time. Then we all went for a walk in this little park called Gethsemane.

But you were still with Jesus.

So far, yeah. Jesus went off on his own for a little while, and we all had trouble staying awake. He had to keep coming over and waking me up, but yeah, we were all still with him then, even when the mob arrived.

Tell us about the mob.

Well, there was this whole pile of soldiers with armor and javelins and torches, the whole bit — like they just walked off some movie set. And leading the bunch up the hill was Judas Iscariot. I thought at first that Judas had gotten some of the soldiers over to our side. It would've been great to have some bodyguards; things were getting pretty tense. And Judas was smart like that, good at organizing. He was our treasurer, you know. But as soon as Judas gave Jesus a hello kiss (we do that kind of thing over here), the mob went on the attack. Turns out Judas was some kind of double agent.

And then this is the point at which you left Jesus.

Did worse than that, if you must know, but not yet. I was all gung-ho at first. I had a sword with me. You don't go walking around Jerusalem at night unarmed, especially around Passover time. Too many out-of-towners, and too many Romans. So I pulled out the sword and took a swipe at this guy Malchus who works for the High Priest. Great aim, too, if I must say so myself. Cut his ear right off.

I wasn't aware that the arrest of Jesus involved violence.

Not much. That was it, really. Jesus told me to put the sword way and I did. Then he told the soldiers that he'd go peacefully if they let all of us go, so they put the cuffs on him and drug him off.

And then you ran away.

Most of the guys did. I didn't. And John didn't either. We faked like that's what we were doing, but then we snuck along behind the soldiers, hiding in the bushes, waiting to see where they took him. If Judas can play double agent, then John and I could do some spying of our own.

So where did you end up going?

We went to the High Priest's house — Caiaphas. John ran up ahead and caught up with Jesus, and they let John in, because he knew some of the people there. I think he even met the High Priest himself a couple of times. John talked to one of the maids later, and she let me into the courtyard.

I don't understand why you say you let Jesus down. It sounds like you were as supportive as you could have been.

I'm getting to that. The maid says to me, "Oh, you're with that Jesus guy they just drug in here." And I'm still into the spy thing, didn't want to blow my cover, so I lied, and said I didn't know what she was talking about. And then I'm standing in the courtyard after she lets me in, warming myself by the fire, and the soldiers keep at me. One guy said, "You gotta be with that troublemaker Jesus. You have the same accent like he does." And another one goes, "Yeah, didn't I see you in

Gethsemane?" And I know he did, 'cause I definitely saw him there. But I keep saying, "No, no, I never even heard of Jesus," and then the rooster crows, and the sun comes up, and it's morning and Jesus was right. Again. I turned my back on him, over and over.

That's certainly understandable.

No, it's not. John stayed with him. Some of the women were there. Even his mother stood by him. As hard as it would have been for us, it would have been a million times worse for her. But nine of the others who were with Jesus on that last night and I ran and hid. We're still hiding.

Yet you called us this morning to set up this interview.

Things have changed. I don't think we're going to be hiding out much longer. This morning we woke up to a frantic pounding on the door. We thought it was going to be the police coming to get us, but it was Mary Magdalene, who stayed with Jesus the whole time. She had just run like a maniac back from the tomb. She went there as soon as the Sabbath was over so she could finish embalming Jesus, but when she got there, the body was gone. Then she said that Jesus was alive. We thought she was hallucinating. You know, wishful thinking, anxiety attacks, something like that.

Could she prove what she said?

We didn't wait around for that. John and I took off like a shot and headed for the tomb. John got there first, he's a lot younger you know, but he got to the door of the tomb and froze. I pushed him aside and went in and, sure enough, it was empty.

The Roman authorities are claiming that their guards fell asleep, and that the body was stolen.

Didn't happen. The body wasn't stolen. Jesus is alive.

You told our producer on the phone this morning that you weren't sure if that was true.

I wasn't sure this morning. But just before I left to come here and meet your cameraman, we had a visit. Jesus came to us. Don't know how he did it. The doors were locked tight, but there he was.

Is he still there, and might he be available for an interview?

Don't know where he is now. After a while, he just wasn't there anymore.

Pardon my saying so, but are you sure that *this* isn't just a hallucination brought on by anxiety or wishful thinking?

Jesus pulled up a chair and ate with us. Hallucinations don't move furniture. Wishful thinking doesn't chew fish. Jesus is alive.

This is astounding news. This must be a very confusing time for you. What will you do now?

This isn't a confusing time at all. Things have never been clearer. I didn't understand half of the things Jesus said to me at the time. It's all coming together now. He once said he'd make us fish for people, and I'm thinking, "What's up with that? Are we supposed to put a sandwich on the end of a line and cast it out into the street?" But I understand how. The hook is the cross, and Jesus is the bait. What am I going to do now? I'm going to go back to work. I've got some fishing to do.

Thank you, Peter. A truly fascinating story.

You're certainly welcome.

Incredible developments this morning. We will continue our coverage as we interview one of the more colorful characters in this affair, and one whose role has apparently just gotten larger than we expected — Mary of Magdala. Good night.

Interview 4

Mary Magdalene

Luke 8:1-3; 1 John 1:1-3; Matthew 27:55-61

Good evening. Jesus of Nazareth has burst into public consciousness and excited the popular imagination in recent times. But does the common image of Jesus as a homeless, penniless, itinerant street preacher and miracle worker go far enough? Is the picture of Jesus' followers as a never-changing group of a dozen men truly accurate, or is the reality more complex? Joining us tonight is someone who challenges that image, Mary of Magdala.

Good evening, Mary.

Hi.

Thank you for taking time to be with us tonight.

No sweat.

Mary, if we could get to the point. Many people have found it surprising to learn that one of Jesus' apostles was a woman.

That surprises me, too. What are you talking about? I know the apostles pretty well, and they're all men. Beards, deep voices, won't ask for directions — they're definitely all men.

But aren't you one of the twelve apostles?

No, I am a disciple of Jesus. I traveled with him, but I wasn't one of the ones we called "the twelve." Well, we're down to eleven now.

So traveling from town to town in the countryside there would be thirteen men and you?

First off, I'm not the token "girl." I'm not like Elaine from _Seinfeld_. When Jesus went around, there weren't just the twelve who went with him. A lot of his followers literally followed. There was a whole pack of us, and many were women.

Did Jesus find it awkward to have a number of women traveling in the group?

I honestly don't think he even noticed.

He didn't notice you were there?

No, of course he knew we were there. Jesus noticed everybody. It's just, well, it's almost like he didn't notice that we were women.

I'm not sure I follow.

You know how it is when you meet somebody new, or even when you just see somebody, the first thing you notice is if they are a woman or a man? It's automatic. You don't even think about it. Just "bing," it's there in your head, so when you talk to that person, you talk to them one way for a man, one way for a woman.

I suppose.

No, it doesn't make you a chauvinist or anything. It's just something we all do. Except for Jesus. It's like that "bing" never went off in his head. You weren't a woman to him, or a man, just a person. When Jesus would talk to you, he'd talk straight to your soul.

Then why aren't the women as well-known? Yours is the only name we have heard.

Not every name gets remembered, but that doesn't make those people less important. Jesus sent seventy people out in pairs to teach and spread the good news. How many of them can you name?

Uh, I'm sorry. I don't have that information in front of me.

That's right, you don't. Just like you don't have the names of the other women. There's a bunch of us: there's Susanna, and the other Mary, the one married to Clopas; a lot of Marys. Sometimes even Jesus' mother Mary, but mostly at the end, and oh, a lot of others. Joanna ...

Yes, that name I believe we have heard. She's the one who has royal connections, is she not?

Royal connections? Not hardly. Her husband Chuza works for Herod, the big sell-out, but he's the butler. He might wash the royal dishes, but that's about it.

Oh.

See, that's why you've never heard of any of the women. You heard of Joanna by mistake; someone thought she was royalty. If she hadn't been mistaken for somebody famous, you wouldn't have heard of her either. Royalty? That's rich. She's gonna love that one. Joanna, are you watching? Is that a hoot or what? The women kept a lower profile than the men. The men were out running around, telling the world about Jesus, casting out demons, doing crowd control, front line stuff that gets noticed.

And the women worked more behind the scenes then?

Yeah, that's right. But we were able to help out in a way that the men couldn't.

And what way was that?

Money.

Money? You offered financial help?

Where do you think the money came from? Even wandering around from town to town, camping outside half of the time, even that you can't do for free. Lots of times people would give us stuff, but that wasn't consistent. Some of us women have a little bit of money, and that's how we contribute to the cause, that and by sticking with Jesus no matter what.

How did you first meet Jesus?

The same way most of the other women did. Most of us are people who were sick or who had other problems. And Jesus changed our lives.

Why the name Magdalene?

Because there are so many Marys. It made it easier for us to know who Jesus was talking to if he gave us little nicknames. They call me Magdalene, because that's where I'm from, Magdala.

Where is Magdala located?

I see you don't have that information in front of you, either. Magdala is right on the Sea of Galilee, on the west side. It's a pretty big city. I'm surprised you've not heard of it. It's famous for its salt business, one of the most important ports in the whole industry.

Which accounts for your somewhat "salty" past.

That was totally uncalled for. You didn't make cracks like that to Peter, or even to Pilate.

You're right; I apologize.

I know there are a lot of rumors out there about me — about how I got my money, a lot of questions about my morals — but they're just rumors. There's no proof. Go and look through your whole Bible, cover to cover, and you won't find anything about my past that's "salty." I'm going on *Oprah* tomorrow; you can bet she won't bring that up.

Yes, Ms. Magdalene, we certainly don't want to be involved in spreading rumors.

Not that my past was perfect. It's just that it really doesn't matter anymore. Jesus changed my life.

You said before that a lot of the women who followed Jesus had been healed by him.

Everybody who follows Jesus does it because he changed their lives. In my case, well, it may not make much sense to your audience.

Please do go on. What happened in your case?

Those of you in the West don't think in these terms, so this will probably sound weird to you, but Jesus changed my life by casting demons out of me.

Demons?

See, I told you; it's not how you Westerners are used to thinking. But, yes, demons. Seven of them.

41

What were these demons?

Well, it's not that easy. Let's just say that the things that used to haunt me don't anymore. The things in my life that used to hold me back, that kept me from being all that I am supposed to be — those things are gone. Jesus changed my life.

I understand that you were with Jesus during his crucifixion.

I couldn't leave him. Most everyone did, all the guys except John. He stayed, and some of us women stayed — most of them "Marys" again. Jesus' own mother was there. We were standing right under the cross at first, but after a little while, the soldiers made us back up: said we were causing a scene. They're killing people on phone poles, and we're the ones causing the scene! I couldn't leave. I wished I was up there on that cross with him. I died that day. I kept breathing, but I died.

What happened after the crucifixion?

I stayed. He screamed; I cried. He stopped moving; I froze. They speared him in the side, and my heart bled. Finally they took him down. Some guy, Joseph of somewhere, said that he was a follower of Jesus, too, though I'd never seen him before in my life. He volunteered the use of his family vault to bury Jesus in. I followed along and watched that, too. After that it's kind of a blur 'til the next day. I remember having to be dragged away from the tomb, but I don't really remember going home.

What happened the next day?

Nothing. The next day was the Sabbath, so that's what you have to do — nothing. So we just paced, planning what we would do the next day, soon as it was daylight. Actually, we weren't even supposed to be pacing. You know, on the Sabbath you're supposed to count your steps.

What were you planning to do?

Why, finish the burial, of course. All they had time to do on Friday was wrap Jesus in a sheet. That's not good enough. So we had all this stuff lined up — potpourri, kinda. About 100 pounds of it. A ton. We were going to give him a nice burial, like he deserved.

And then the next morning you finished the funeral.

(*Slowly smiling*) **No.**

No?

No. We didn't have to. The grave was empty.

We have heard that some are saying that Jesus rose from the dead.

Yeah, *I'm saying* he rose from the dead. It's true, I saw him. And don't give me any of this "hysterical woman" stuff or I'll deck you.

I wouldn't think of it. Where did you see him?

In the garden. Right outside of the vault. When we got close, we saw that the tomb was open. There had been this huge rock in front of it.

So what did you do?

I went and told the twelve. Well, eleven. And Peter and John ran straight for the tomb.

But you said that you saw Jesus personally.

I went back to the tomb. And when I got there, Peter and John had already been there and gone, but there were these two

guys in white suits. They're sitting in the tomb, where the body is supposed to be. They said something about looking in the wrong place. And I panicked, of course, and I turned around, and shot out of the tomb, and there's this guy there. Like *right* there. And he's tall, and I'm looking down and wiping my eyes, and I didn't know who he was. I thought he was one of those guys that does the lawn. And I said, "If you moved him, tell me where you put him, 'cause we brought all the stuff to finish the burial," and then he speaks. He says, "Mary." And I look up, and it's Jesus.

So what are you planning to do now?

Same thing I'm doing right this minute. Telling people about Jesus. About how he can change your life. About how he rose from the dead. First I told the twelve (eleven). And now I'm telling you. Jesus sees you for who you are. He talks right to your soul. And he's alive!

Thank you for joining us, and thank you for telling your story.

You're welcome. That's what I do now. That's what I'll always do. Tell that story.

Good night.

Peace.

The story of Jesus of Nazareth continues to grow, becoming more amazing by the hour. Join us next time as we interview John, the youngest member of the group Jesus called "the twelve."

John

Job 19:23-25; Acts 8:14-17; John 21:20-25

Good evening. We continue tonight to investigate the strange circumstances surrounding the death and burial of Jesus of Nazareth. Who was this man? Was he a revolutionary or a prophet? A faithful interpreter of the Holy Scriptures, or a radical with no regard for tradition? And was his body stolen, or was he somehow brought back to life? Joining us tonight, live from Jerusalem, is a man who knew Jesus very closely; the Apostle John, the only member of the group known as "the twelve" who was also witness to the crucifixion of Jesus.

Thank you, John. You are someone I've looked forward to talking with.

You're welcome. Don't end your sentence with a preposition. You want to say "I've looked forward to talking with you."

Right. Sorry.

I don't mean to be rude. It's just that I've been much more aware of words lately.

John, you are perhaps uniquely suited to answer the question millions have been asking. Just who was this Jesus of Nazareth? Or perhaps we should say who "is" this Jesus?

Both of those work. Jesus was; Jesus is. "Will be" works, too. Jesus is a difficult person on which to pin a verb tense.

Because you're not certain whether he is dead or not?

No, not that. I have no doubt about that. I saw him die. I looked at his corpse. Later I saw him alive. He's definitely alive, but he was also definitely dead. Jesus was alive; Jesus is alive. Existed always before; will exist always after. See what I mean? He's kind of hard on grammar.

I see. Well, verb tenses aside, how would you describe Jesus? Prophet, revolutionary, religious conservative, religious radical?

Uh, yes.

What do you mean, "Yes." Those terms are contradictory.

No, they're just not very complete. Jesus was, uh, *is* definitely a prophet. He spoke the word of God, brought God's will to bear on the real world, here and now, looked ahead to what God is going to do. That's a prophet. But he is/was also a revolutionary. He certainly turns things upside down. He changes how we see power, how we see God, how we see everything.

We have heard reports of his turning tables upside down in the Temple.

Well, that's not exactly what I had in mind, but, yes, he did do that.

We understand that it was a very public display of anger, for no apparent reason. Perhaps you could explain, for the benefit of our viewers, why Jesus engaged in such an act of vandalism.

It was a statement. Everything that Jesus did said something. It's almost as if you were listening to his actions rather than watching them. Yes, he was very angry, but he had a reason to be. I would hardly call what he did vandalism. He was acting against activities that had no place in the Temple.

For our non-Jewish viewers, let me clarify. Worship at the Temple often includes animal sacrifices. The animals to be sacrificed must first be inspected by priests, and can be refused if the animal has even the slightest imperfection. Therefore, to save someone bringing an animal hundreds of miles, only to be told at the last minute that the animal is unusable, pre-approved animals are sold in the temple courtyard. There are even kiosks set up where a foreign traveler could convert his currency into temple coin.

That was a little wordy, but accurate.

And Jesus attacked the legitimate businessmen, who were working with full approval of the temple authorities.

As I said before, it was a statement. It wasn't about whether or not the people selling doves had a vending license. It was about people getting caught up in silly regulations and fixating on whether someone's goat had a pimple on its left ear, instead of focusing on the glory of God. People were trying to buy off God, and these so-called legitimate businessmen were encouraging this nonsense.

So it was an attack on the temple practices as much as an attack on the merchants?

Yes. It wasn't about goats or buildings, or exchange rates; it was always about true worship, and hearing the word of God.

But Jesus threatened to destroy the Temple itself.

Jesus is not Osama Bin-Laden. He wasn't going to blow anything up.

The quote was, I believe, "Destroy this temple, and in three days I will raise it up." Are you saying that Jesus has been misquoted?

No, he said it all right. I've been thinking a great deal about that these past few days, actually, and I've come to believe that he wasn't really talking about the Temple.

"Destroy *this* temple, and in ..."

(*Interrupting*) I know the quote. But the temple he was talking about wasn't Jerusalem's number one tourist attraction. He was talking about himself. The temple of his body. It was destroyed, but in three days, God raised him up again.

Jesus was comparing himself to the Temple?

Yes, I believe so. It makes sense. The Temple was where people would go to meet God. But all that's changed now. This is a way in which Jesus is truly revolutionary. Heaven and earth don't meet in some architectural wonder downtown here. Heaven and earth meet in Jesus.

That's quite a claim.

I realize that. But it's true. It's who Jesus is.

And that brings us back to our original question: Who is, or was, Jesus of Nazareth?

I've been developing this fascination for words lately, as I mentioned before. I've been trying to remember things that Jesus said, both verbally and in his actions. I've been writing little lists of things. Maybe someday I'll write it all down, although I don't think I could ever really get it all. If the whole world were just one big library, it still wouldn't be big enough to hold everything. One of the lists I've been making is a list of ways that Jesus answered that question.

What Jesus said about who he is?

Yes. That would probably be the best way to answer your question.

Do you have the list with you?

I do. Your producer here insisted on typing it into the tele-prompter, but that's not really necessary. I know them all by heart.

Very well, then. Who did Jesus say — who does he say — that he is? Uh, that he was?

See, he's just hard on grammar.

You're telling me.

Some of these he said over and over, at different times, worded slightly differently. I'll skip over the more repetitive ones.

Thank you.

Well, he said, "I am the Messiah."

Messiah.

From the Hebrew, *Meshiach*. *Christos* in Greek. You would say something like, *oil-smeared* or *anointed*. It means God's cho-sen person.

Okay.

Then, "I am the Bread of Life."

He's bread?

He's what you need to keep going. He's God's way of taking care of us. Sometimes he put it, "I am the living bread come down from heaven."

Very interesting.

More than interesting. This isn't just academic. This is the meaning of life we're talking about here.

Of course. Please go on.

"I am the light of the world."

Light of the world?

Jesus, that is, not me.

I understand.

Jesus makes it so we can see what's really going on, what really matters. Let's see. He also says, "I am the one who testifies for myself."

What does that mean?

That only Jesus can truly define who Jesus is. It's because of that one that I'm reading this list to you. We can't put Jesus into a pigeonhole. He's so far beyond anything else in human experience. "I am the good Shepherd" and "I am the gate of the sheepfold."

I'm not clear on the "gate" one.

Jesus gathers God's people, protects them, and keeps them together like a shepherd.

That makes it sound as if Jesus is claiming to be God.

He gets more to the point. Listen to these: "I am from above" and "I am not of this world." "I am the way, the truth, and the life." "I am the resurrection and the life." "I am in the Father." "I am the Son of God." "I am ..."

Uh, John, in the interest of time, could you just pick one of these sayings that, in your mind, best sums up who Jesus is?

Out of the things that he said?

Yes, if you would please.

I am.

(*Pause*) I'm sorry, John, we seem to be having some trouble with the transmission, we didn't hear the end of that last sentence.

That's it, just "I am."

That's sort of obvious, don't you think?

Yes, *I* think so. But you'd be surprised how many people don't catch that one.

Don't catch what?

Oh, I'm sorry, I just assumed ... You know, when God spoke to Moses out of the burning bush?

Yes?

Well, Moses asked God what his name was, who he should say had sent him, and God said, "I am who I am. Tell them that 'I am' has sent you."

So Jesus is saying that he is God?

He is.

But what are you saying about him? You have reported what Jesus said of himself. What do you think? Who would you say that Jesus is?

I said before that only Jesus can truly define who Jesus is. Nothing I could say would really be adequate. There will always be more to Jesus than I could tell you, but since you insist, I'll take a crack at it. I've become fascinated with words of late, and here's why. Jesus is the Word of God.

How is that possible?

I have no idea. But it's true. In the beginning was the Word, and the Word was with God, and the Word was God. He was in the beginning with God; all things were made through him, and without him was not anything made that was made. In him was life. And the Word became flesh and dwelt among us. That's who Jesus is.

Thank you, John. I don't know if that makes things any clearer, but you've certainly given us something to think about.

You're welcome. I hope you do think about it. I hope your audience does, too. Peace be with you.

Live from Jerusalem, that was the Apostle John. Our interview with John was to be the last in this series of conversations about the crucifixion of Jesus. But we have just received word this afternoon of an informant within the Roman military who promises, in his words, to "blow the lid off" the conflicting claims made by the followers of Jesus and the empire. Join us next week on *Dateline: Jerusalem.*

The Centurion

2 Timothy 2:1-7; Psalm 27:1-4; Matthew 27:45-54

Good evening. We continue tonight with a different look at the controversial story of Jesus of Nazareth. The two sides in this heavily-contended event: the followers of Jesus, who insist that Jesus rose from the dead after his execution by crucifixion, and an unlikely coalition of Roman Imperial Officials and the Office of the High Priest of Israel. This coalition has been contending that the Roman guard placed outside of the tomb of Jesus was derelict in their duty, allowing the followers of Jesus to come and steal Jesus' body and thus perpetrate the hoax of his resurrection. Joining us tonight, under condition of anonymity, is a Roman officer who professes to know the complete, inside story.

Thank you for joining us.

Yes, sir.

You have agreed to speak to us only if we could assure complete anonymity.

That is correct.

Why is that?

Because I don't want anyone to know who I am.

Clearly. But why is that?

If my superiors know who I am, it'll be just that much easier for them to kill me.

We wouldn't want that.

I wouldn't either. That would be bad.

Why do you think they would kill you?

Because I'm going to tell you things they don't want you to hear. Telling you this is treason.

Why did you come to us if it is so dangerous?

I'm an officer in the Imperial Infantry. We are expected to be obedient to the emperor — "for the Senate and the People of Rome" and all that. But we are also expected to act with honor. I expect that of myself. There is a cover-up going on, and it's just not right. Dishonorable. The Senate and the People of Rome, and even all you barbarians, need to know what's really going on.

You want to bring the truth to light.

No! (*Covers face with arm*) **Whatever you do, don't turn a light on!**

Sorry, I meant ... You have come here to tell us the truth.

Right. No more lies.

Thank you. Before we go on — we obviously can't use your name, so how should we address you?

Just call me Centurion.

Centurion?

54

That's my rank. It means I'm in command of 100 men.

Okay, Centurion. Sir, if you could tell us of your involvement in the Jesus case.

I first saw Jesus when he was brought into the Praetorium.

Could you please describe what a praetorium is for the benefit of our viewers?

The Praetorium is the HQ of the Roman presence in Jerusalem. The Governor has offices there, court is held there, and other government functions; and of course, there is a barracks for the Imperial Legions.

How many Roman troops are stationed in Jerusalem?

I'm here to blow the whistle on a cover-up, but that doesn't mean I'm giving out classified military information.

Sorry, I was just exercising the public's right to know.

This is the Roman Empire, there's no sissy first amendment here.

Of course not. Tell us about that meeting with Jesus.

He was brought to the Praetorium by the chief priest's guards, but they didn't come in, something about getting all unholy if they came into our building. I don't know what that's supposed to mean. They have some weird ideas. So his Excellency the governor had to keep going in and out of the compound, trying to figure out what exactly they wanted us to do with Jesus.

And what did they want you to do with Jesus?

Kill him, I suppose.

You're not sure?

Most likely that's what they were after. That's what ended up happening. As I said, they were outside; I was inside. Governor Pilate kept asking Jesus questions and then going out and talking to the high priest's people, then asking Jesus more questions. He was getting pretty frustrated.

Jesus was getting frustrated?

No, not him. Pilate. Jesus was calm as could be. Stubborn, yes. He would barely answer Pilate. But frustrated? Nothing. No anger, no fear. It was weird. I think the Governor thought it was weird, too, because he even asked Jesus if he understood what he could do to him. What Pilate could do to Jesus, I mean.

Did he understand?

I don't know how to answer you. If anything, he understood more than that. He told Pilate that he, the Governor, couldn't be doing anything unless his God allowed it.

What did the Governor think of that?

It freaked him out. That and he got some message from his wife, and he started pacing like a panther. Pilate just wanted Jesus out of there. So he thought he'd punish Jesus a little, let the chief priests know he was taking them seriously, and then let him go. So he turned Jesus over to us.

And what did you do?

It might surprise your ah, audience, but there can be an ugly side to military life.

Do tell.

Yes, sir. You'd be surprised. We took Jesus and gave him the customary forty lashes. (Actually we only give 39 lashes, just in case we lost count somewhere. You wouldn't want to go over.) But before we got to that, some of the boys had a little fun.

What kind of fun do you mean?

I was in on it, too, sorry to say. Well, we heard he was supposed to be some kind of prophet, so we blindfolded him, then stood around in a circle and took turns beating on him, seeing if he could use his prophet power to say who hit him.

Was he able to guess correctly?

What are you talking about? Of course he didn't guess correctly! He didn't guess at all. He just stood there and took it. You could see he was hurting. We're not little guys, and we really let him have it, but he never said anything.

Sounds pretty brutal.

It gets worse. We overheard Governor Pilate say something about him being a king, so we wrapped him in a purple tablecloth, and put a stick in his hand, and pretended to bow down like you do to a king, only every time we came up from the bow, we punched him square in the face. Then someone got the idea to make a crown for him out of some briars. There are some pretty nasty ones that grow over here, and we smashed it down on his head until he was so bloody his own mother couldn't have recognized him.

But Jesus was not let go after that.

No. By this time there was a mob outside, and Pilate took Jesus out to them, all dressed up like we had him, but they just started screaming for Jesus' blood.

Governor Pilate himself told us the chief priests had goaded the crowd into that.

I don't know about that. That's outside, remember? I was in.

Of course.

So Pilate came back in wiping his hands on his toga and swearing up a blue streak. Then he points over to us soldiers and says, "Do what they say." And we can hear the crowd outside: "Crucify him, crucify him!"

So that's what you did.

Yes, sir.

Tell us about the crucifixion.

Crucifixion is never pretty, but this was worse than usual. We nailed him to the cross. Right through his hands and feet. Most always, we tie the poor saps to the crosses. Not him. Nails about this long. (*Hold hands about nine inches apart.*)

Did you see the whole crucifixion?

That's part of the job. I'm at four or five crucifixions a week, sometimes a lot more. Several at a time. Mostly, you don't watch the whole thing beginning to end. It can take a week or more for some of them to die. You pull guard duty at Golgotha (that's where we crucify here at Jerusalem), maybe one watch every couple of days. Because of the politics surrounding Jesus — this being a big Jewish holiday with a lot of troublemakers in town for the occasion — a number of us were assigned to stick with Jesus till the end.

And so you were there for the whole crucifixion.

It was very short, mostly because he was already in pretty bad shape when we put him up there. Jesus died right away, within a couple of hours. But it seemed like forever.

What do you mean?

Well, at the start of it, we were still horsing around, drawing straws for Jesus' clothes, divvying up his stuff right in front of him, like we always do. But then we noticed it was getting dark.

And time for the night watch.

No. **It was lunchtime. But it sure didn't look like it. It just kept getting darker. Not cloudy, just dark.**

That's strange.

That's not all of it. After a couple of hours, Jesus lets out this big yell. He had mumbled some things before, I wasn't really paying attention, but he lets out this scream and then there's this earthquake. And then he stops moving, and so does the ground. I saw one of the other soldiers go up and poke him with his javelin. Just kept jabbing at him, until there's all this blood, and Jesus doesn't move. And then it's light again.

The sun came back out?

No, the sun hadn't gone anywhere; it just quit shining. But the light comes back and I'm thinking: "This really was a Son of God."

Are you saying that you became a believer in Jesus at that point?

No, I don't think so. I wouldn't have known what to believe about him, except that it looked like the gods sure weren't happy that we killed him.

And then Jesus was buried.

**Yes, sir. They were in an awful hurry. A big holiday was start-
ing and the Jewish people weren't allowed to touch any dead
bodies once it started or else ... I don't know what. They just
weren't supposed to. So they had to get him buried before sundown, because that's when the holiday started. I thought that
was kind of funny, since it had already been dark once that
day, but they were in a big rush. Someone loaned his tomb,
temporary-like, until permanent arrangements could be figured out. So on the Governor's orders, once they put the body
in the tomb, we closed it up with a rock, like those Jewish tombs
do, but we also sealed it with wax, and stood guard.**

What was the purpose of the wax?

**So you could tell if the tomb had been messed with. If the wax
was broken, someone had been in there.**

Couldn't someone reseal it with new wax?

We would know.

How would you be able to tell?

**We use a special seal to make a mark in the wax. Details are
classified. But it doesn't matter. No one sneaks past the Roman Infantry.**

But Pilate says the guards all fell sleep and the body was stolen.

He's lying.

You say this about the Imperial Governor of Judea?

**Yes, sir. It's treason, I know. That's why I'm hiding in the dark
like this. I could get killed for telling you this. I *will* get killed if
they figure out who I am.**

60

How do we know you're telling the truth?

If I fell asleep on guard duty, they'd have killed me already. No one fell asleep, they just told us to say that we did, then paid us to keep quiet.

Then what are you saying happened?

We saw this light in the middle of the night, and these two guys. Not normal guys. Wearing white clothes, but ... well, I can't really describe them. They rolled the stone back while we just stood there in shock. And then he came out of the tomb.

The dead Jesus walked out of the tomb.

No! You make it sound like a zombie movie! Dead people don't walk. He wasn't dead, not anymore. He walked out of the grave just like you walk out of your house in the morning.

And what did you and the other soldiers do?

We ran. These were brave men. I know most of them pretty well, but we all ran for our lives. I haven't seen any of them since. We're all being transferred, split up. I doubt I'll see any of them again. But I've been watching your show. I heard what Pilate said, the liar. And I heard those other people, too. I had to come and set the record straight. Jesus is alive.

There you've heard it from an inside source: the Empire's story of grave robbers and a hoax is itself an elaborate cover-up. What conclusions can we draw from this, and from the other interviews in this series? Only one: Jesus of Nazareth is alive! Good night, and have an eternal tomorrow.